Designed to Fail

Canada's Broken
Firearm Prohibition Order System
and How to Fix It

by

Christopher di Armani

ISBN: 978-1-988938-52-3

Published By:
Botanie Valley Productions Inc.
PO Box 507
Lytton, BC V0K 1Z0
http://BotanieValleyProductions.com

Dedication

This book is dedicated to my sweet and loving wife Lynda.

Without her unwavering support none of this would be possible.

Acknowledgments

I thank Dennis Young for his invaluable research.

Designed to Fail would not... **could not** be as complete without his assistance.

I am so grateful for Dennis' willingness to find and send me the various ATIP responses I needed, and for his feedback on early versions of this manuscript despite his own serious health challenges.

Thank you, Dennis. I couldn't have written this without you!

Table of Contents

Introduction

In the pages ahead I will make the case for a new firearm prohibition order system – one modeled after the United Kingdom's Management of Sexual and Violent Offenders (MOSOVO) Units.

Unlike Canada, the United Kingdom created specialized police units whose sole purpose is to track and search sex offenders and violent offenders prohibited from possessing weapons to ensure they comply with the terms of their Harm Prevention Orders.

The rational is simple.

Common sense dictates we devote our scarce police resources to those individuals who pose the greatest risk to public safety – violent offenders with Firearm Prohibition Orders registered against them – yet these are the people Canada's legislators completely ignore despite their claims of keeping Canadians safe.

Under our current legislation, the only government agency notified when an individual is prohibited from possessing firearms is the RCMP Canadian Firearms Program (CFP).

Why?

So the CFP can revoke that individual's Possession and Acquisition Licence (PAL).

If the individual does not have a PAL, they are totally ignored by our justice system.

Individuals convicted of violent offences who are prohibited from possessing firearms are a proven danger to public safety, yet:

☒ **No police agency** in Canada tracks individuals with Firearm Prohibition Orders registered against them.

☒ There is **no legal requirement** for police to track individuals with Firearm Prohibition Orders registered against them.

☒ **There is no legal ability** to routinely track or check on individuals with Firearm Prohibition Orders registered against them to ensure compliance.

☒ **There is no legal obligation** for individuals with Firearm Prohibition Orders to notify police when they move to a new residence. Police have no idea where these people are.

Common sense also dictates we shouldn't waste our scarce police resources on federally-licenced, RCMP-vetted gun owners who are, statistically, less of a threat to public safety than the general public and serving police officers, yet these are the people upon whom Canada's legislators focus all their energy in their quest for public safety.

If we truly want to enhance public safety, there are far better ways to achieve this worthy goal.

For those who don't know, to legally own firearms in Canada you must apply for and be issued a firearm Possession and Acquisition Licence (PAL) from the RCMP Canadian Firearms Program.

Once issued a PAL, a licenced firearm owner:

☑ **Must** notify the Canadian Firearms Program of their change of address within 30 days or face up to 2 years in prison.

☑ **Must** request and receive permission (*Authorization to Transport*) from the Canadian Firearms Program to move their private property (*Restricted and Prohibited firearms*) from their old address to their new address.

☑ **Must** request and receive permission (*Authorization to Transport*) from the Canadian Firearms Program to take their Restricted firearms to and from federally licenced shooting ranges.

☑ **Must** request and receive permission (*Authorization to Transport*) from the Canadian Firearms Program to take their Restricted firearms to and from a gunsmith.

☑ Are **Screened Daily** by the RCMP Canadian Firearms Program's Continuous Eligibility Screening Program.[1]

For more information about Canada's strict firearms control system and the many legal requirements for firearm ownership please see:

Appendix 2: A Primer on Canadian Gun Laws.

Governments Fund What They Care About

The Trudeau government, through Minister of Border Security and Organized Crime Reduction Bill Blair, first announced $327.6 million over five years in new federal funding for the *Initiative to Take Action Against Guns and Gangs* in November, 2017.[2]

The Trudeau government repeated this $327 million funding announcement for the next two and a half years, including during their May 1, 2020, press conference banning over 100,000 legally-acquired firearms by Order in Council.

Of this, only $86 million over five years ($17 million per year) is destined for Canada Border Services Agency and the RCMP to stop firearms from being smuggled into Canada – the Number One source of illegal guns for drug dealers and gangs (and the Nova Scotia mass murderer).

Contrast this with the cost of "buying back" firearms from licensed, RCMP-vetted gun owners.

Public Safety Minister Bill Blair said it will cost roughly $600 million to purchase legally-owned guns from licenced gun owners so the federal government can dump these legally-owned firearms into smelters and proudly proclaim they've "done something" about guns.[3]

The Minister's estimate is likely one-third of the actual costs according to the Fraser Institute.[4] Total costs could exceed $1.5 billion. Yes, that's with a "**B**".

It doesn't take a rocket scientist to see where the Liberal government's priorities are – it's not with stopping violent criminals from obtaining illegal guns and committing crimes with them.

The Liberal government's priority is taking guns away from sport shooters, hunters and farmers – statistically the most law-abiding people in the country.

Which brings me back to where I started with this introduction – focusing our scarce resources on those most likely to commit violent offences and threaten public safety – those individuals with Firearm Prohibition Orders registered against them.

As I noted above, the primary purpose of a Firearm Prohibition Order is to notify the RCMP Canadian Firearms Program in case the individual holds a firearms Possession and Acquisition Licence (PAL).

The Canadian Firearms Program uses this information to revoke an individual's firearms licence.

This is the only case where any police agency in Canada pays any attention to individuals prohibited by court order from possessing guns.

When the government's priority is taking legally-owned guns away from federally-licenced RCMP-vetted gun owners, it's easy to understand why Canada's Firearms Prohibition Order system is designed to fail.

Chapter 1

Why Track Violent Offenders With Firearm Prohibition Orders?

The answer to this question should be obvious to everyone with an IQ above zero.

Should be...

Individuals prohibited from possessing firearms by a judge pose the greatest threat to public safety because their risk of re-offending is high. Knowing where these offenders are is critical to ensure they obey their Firearm Prohibition Orders.

According to the 2014 Correctional Service of Canada (CSC) offender population profile, about eight out of 10 male and seven out of 10 female offenders have previous convictions. In the 2013 report, the stats were nine out of 10 men and eight out of 10 women.[5]

An international study of recidivism showed re-conviction rates for prisoners in the United States and United Kingdom were 55% and 72% respectively after five years. After nine years, the U.K. rate rose to 78%.[6]

That same study showed Canada's 2-year re-conviction rate was 41%. While this is better than many other countries, it still means almost half of all people convicted of a crime will leave prison to commit more crimes.

The 2018 RCMP Commissioner of Firearms Report says on December 31, 2018, there were 459,538 individuals prohibited from possessing firearms in Canada.[7]

Using Canada's 2-year re-conviction rate as the low end and Canada's 2014 CSC population profile data on previous convictions as the high end, between 188,410 and 367,630 individuals currently prohibited from possessing firearms could be violating their Firearm Prohibition Orders today.

Those frightening numbers are all the more terrifying when news reports show only 29 of these re-offenders are, on average, caught and disarmed (again) each month.[8]

Through one of many his Freedom of Information requests, firearm researcher Dennis Young learned that from 2014 to 2018 (the latest year stats are available) police arrested 5,550 criminals who were already prohibited from possessing firearms – an average of 1,110 per year.[9]

The logical group of people to track and check on regularly would be "convicted criminals who have been prohibited from owning firearms, both because of their high risk to re-offend (i.e. acquire firearms illegally and use firearms in the commission of a subsequent offence) and because of their past firearms convictions they represent a higher risk to both police and public safety."[10]

The operating principle of our Liberal government is fundamentally flawed, as is that of the many groups advocating banning guns from licensed gun owners.

Their thinking goes like this:

> *Guns cause violent crime and murder.*

> *When you believe guns cause crime and murder, why would you go after individual people?*

> *That's completely illogical.*

> *Public safety is enhanced by removing the hated object from society, not the violent criminal who uses it to injure or kill someone.*

Utter nonsense.

People, not pieces of metal, commit violence and endanger the safety of us all.

A loaded firearm left on a table will not harm anyone until a human being with evil intent in their heart picks up that firearm and uses it.

Biblically, this is called the *Doctrine of Total Depravity*.

> *Genesis 6:5*   Then the LORD saw that the wickedness of man was great on the earth, and that every intent of the thoughts of his heart were only evil continually.

One proof of this doctrine is Derek Chauvin, the now-former Minneapolis police officer who murdered George Floyd on camera, seemingly unconcerned his actions were recorded while the world watched in horror.

The May and June 2020 riots across North America (they're not lawful protests against anything) prove this doctrine beyond any reasonable doubt.

How else do you explain the mobs of criminals burning down businesses[11] and police stations[12], looting stores[13], destroying vehicles[14], beating people mercilessly and murdering them[15] for daring to try and stop these opportunistic law-breakers?

They are not protesting a brutal police murder of an innocent man. They're acting out their basic human depravity for all the world to see and they don't care who they injure or kill along the way.

This is true for our "garden variety" criminals with firearm prohibition orders against them as well.

Recidivism

If the focus is truly on preventing violent crime, then why ignore those people who are most likely to commit violent crimes?

Spending two to three times as much money on taking guns away from the people *least likely* to cause anyone harm – federally-licensed RCMP-vetted firearm owners – than we do on stopping those individuals who present the greatest threat to public safety – violent offenders with firearm prohibition orders – is the textbook definition of insane.

Insane:[16]

> 1 : exhibiting a severely disordered state of mind

> 2 : unable to think in a clear or sensible way

It is not *sensible* to expend more resources on those least likely to endanger public safety than on those who are proven threats to it.

The doctrine of human depravity means a person intent on using violence, as proven by a conviction and the imposition of a firearms prohibition order, is far more likely to commit another violent offence in the future.

In corrections language, this is called recidivism – the tendency to relapse into previous criminal behavior.

How we deal with recidivism is multifaceted, to be sure, but one of the ways to combat this problem is by helping these individuals change their lives for the better through education and training.

Unfortunately, all the social programs in the world will not help the person who doesn't want to change their lives for the better.

For those people, we need interdiction programs to ensure compliance with court orders and probation terms.

We need specialized police units, like the United Kingdom's Management of Sexual and Violent Offenders Units, who provide education and training to offenders, but also perform meaningful compliance checks to ensure they abide by the terms of their prevention orders.

We must prioritize our limited police budgets so we spend money on those areas where we can have the greatest impact on public safety.

We also need a federal government with the will to pass legislation to implement this system to ensure Canadians are protected from the most violent offenders in our country.

Chapter 2

How Firearm Prohibition Orders Work in Canada

Overview

When an individual is convicted of a violent offence or another related offence a judge may issue a Firearms Prohibition Order against that individual for a period of a few months to the rest of the offender's life.

The *Criminal Code* provides for three types of prohibition orders:

1. Mandatory Firearm Prohibition Orders (Section 109)[17]
2. Discretionary Firearm Prohibition Orders (Section 110)[18]
3. Preventative Firearm Prohibition Orders (Section 111)[19]

Mandatory Firearm Prohibition Orders apply, as part of a sentence, for all convictions for criminal offences meeting the criteria listed in s. 109(1):[20]

- The use of violence or the threat of use of violence
- Using a firearm in the commission of another offence
- Weapons trafficking
- Criminal harassment with a firearm
- Drug trafficking
- Possession for the purpose trafficking
- Drug smuggling into or out of Canada
- Manufacturing drugs

For a first offence of those listed in s.109(1) a 10-year firearms prohibition order is mandatory. For second and subsequence offences a lifetime firearms prohibition order is mandatory.

Once a mandatory Firearm Prohibition Order is issued the *Criminal Code* does not provide any means to vary or remove it.

Discretionary Firearm Prohibition Orders apply, as part of a sentence, but the judge has discretion to tailor the order specifically to the circumstances of the individual before the courts up to a maximum of 10 years.

There is no minimum duration – which explains why the Nova Scotia killer received a nine-month firearms prohibition which was widely reported in the news. His case was dealt with using the discretionary option.

Unlike mandatory Firearm Prohibition Orders, discretionary orders may be varied should the individual's circumstances change.

A **Preventative Firearm Prohibition Order** allows any peace officer or firearms officer to request a Firearm Prohibition Order against any person if the peace officer or firearms officer believes the prohibition is in the interests of public safety.

There is no requirement for the individual to be charged with or convicted of a crime. So long as the "balance of probabilities", not the much higher "proof beyond a reasonable doubt" required for a conviction, favour the individual be prohibited from possessing firearms, the order will probably be granted.

A provincial court judge may, on application by the person against whom a s.111 discretionary prohibition order is made, revoke the order if the judge is satisfied the circumstances causing the order to be issued no longer exist.

Reporting of Prohibition Orders

Section 89 of the *Firearms Act* identifies who must be notified when a judge issues a firearm prohibition order against an individual.

> **89** Every court, judge or justice that makes, varies or revokes a prohibition order shall have a chief firearms officer informed without delay of the prohibition order or its variation or revocation.[21]

That's it.

The only agency notified when a judge issues a firearms prohibition order against an individual is the Chief Firearms Officer of the province where the conviction took place.

This means the only purpose of a firearms prohibition order is to allow the Canadian Firearms Program to revoke that individual's Possession and Acquisition Licence – if they have one.

The 2018 Commissioner of Firearms Report explains:[22]

> Under section 89 of the *Firearms Act*, every court, judge or justice that orders, varies or revokes a firearms prohibition order must notify the CFO in their jurisdiction. Firearms licence applicant screening includes checking if an applicant is subject to a prohibition order.
>
> A prohibition order prevents an individual from legally possessing a firearm for a specified period of time and results in the refusal of a firearms licence application or the revocation of a firearms licence.

However, under section 113 of the *Criminal Code*, special provisions may be made for an individual, against whom a prohibition order is made, to possess a firearm if they are able to establish to the satisfaction of a competent authority that they require a firearm for the purpose of hunting in order to sustain themselves or their family.

If the individual does not have a Possession and Acquisition Licence (i.e. they are not *"clients"* of the Canadian Firearms Program) that's literally the end of it as far as our justice system is concerned.

Garry Breitkreuz, the former Saskatchewan Member of Parliament responsible for getting rid of the long gun registry, thought this was insane so he questioned Minister of Justice Anne McLellan about it during a meeting of the Standing Committee on Justice, Human Rights, Public Safety and Emergency Preparedness on November 24, 2004:[23]

> **Mr. Garry Breitkreuz**: "The RCMP tell us there are approximately 176,000 criminals who have been prohibited from owning firearms by the courts and there are another 37,000 dangerous persons who have restraining orders against them. Why are these persons, who have been proven to be dangerous, not required to report their change of address to police or even open up their homes to firearms inspection, but completely innocent licensed gun owners are required to? There's just no logic to that, Madam Minister. I'm wondering if you could answer that."

> **Hon. Anne McLellan**: "Mr. Baker, do you want to answer some of those specific questions?"

Mr. Bill Baker: "Yes, Minister. On the change of address, if someone is prohibited from having a firearm in the country they are no longer effectively covered by the *Firearms Act*. The *Firearms Act* only deals with people who own, possess, and use firearms."

Mr. Garry Breitkreuz: "Yes, but that's why I asked the minister, where's the logic?"

Bill Baker: "In terms of firearms officers, they would have no authority to collect information from somebody who is not a client of the program."

Who the RCMP Tracks on CPIC (and who they don't)

On June 7, 2016, Dennis Young received a response to his Access to Information requests regarding who the RCMP tracks via the Canadian Police Information Centre (CPIC) and who they don't.[24]

First, who the RCMP tracks via CPIC.

After a firearms licence is approved, continuous eligibility screening is conducted over the term of the licence. Accordingly, all current holders of firearms licences are recorded in the Canadian Firearms Information System (CFIS).

CFIS automatically checks with the Canadian Police Information Centre (CPIC) every day to determine whether a licence holder has been the subject of an incident report in CPIC.

If a licensed individual is the subject of a police report related to a section 5 event, as per the *Firearms Act*, a report will be automatically sent to the Chief Firearms Officer of the applicant's jurisdiction for review and investigation.

Next, who CPIC does not track.

Dennis Young asked the RCMP for:

(1) the number of convicted violent offenders who have completely served their sentences;
(2) the number of persons prohibited from owning firearms by the courts;
(3) the number of persons released on bail, parole and conditional release;
(4) the number of persons with restraining/protection orders against them;
(5) the number of persons with an outstanding criminal arrest warrant;
(6) the number of persons who have had their firearms license revoked;
(7) the number of firearms license holders currently being investigated as a result of the Continuous Eligibility Program; and
(8) for each group of persons in items (1) to (5), please show the number of persons that currently hold a valid firearms license.

The RCMP's response?

Based on the information provided, a search for records was conducted in the CPIC system. Unfortunately, we were unable to locate records which respond to your request. Please take note, that the CPI Centre is unable to provide answers to the questions asked as the CPIC system is not used for statistical purposes.

On July 26, 2016, Dennis Young received a response to another Access to Information request detailing the types of records and information that can be returned from a CPIC check.[24]

When a person's name is queried in CPIC, the police officer has a wide range of information available to them. The information available on CPIC includes:

- if the person is wanted for any reason
- if the person
  - is violent
  - a known sex offender
  - a known prolific/dangerous/high risk offender
  - is charged with an offence
  - on probation or parole
  - is subject to a restraining order or peace bond
  - is prohibited from possessing firearms
  - is prohibited from driving
  - has a criminal record and all details of it
  - has a firearms licence and all firearms registered to them
  - and much more...

In light of the fact the RCMP doesn't track violent offenders, rapists and sex offenders, the obvious question is, "Why not?"

CPIC contains all the information required to track these offenders.

They simply don't use it.

Designed To Fail

This is why I say the entire Firearm Prohibition Order system is designed to fail.

Once an individual's Possession and Acquisition Licence expires, they are no longer a client of the Canadian Firearms Program and the provisions of the *Firearms Act* no longer apply.

Furthermore, a piece of paper *cannot* and provably *does not* stop a criminal from illegally obtaining a firearm and committing more violent offences[25] with it because, ultimately, that's all a Firearms Prohibition Order is – a piece of useless paper.

Chapter 3

Continuous Eligibility Screening for Licenced Firearm Owners

Section 5 of the *Firearms Act* provides CFOs with guidance to determine if a person is eligible to obtain a new Possession and Acquisition Licence (PAL) or whether they remain eligible to hold that licence.

The following is from the RCMP's Audit of the Canadian Firearms Program continuum of eligibility for firearms licensing, published in February, 2018.[26]

> The *Firearms Act* and its related regulations are the legislative components that govern the administration of the CFP. The Act defines criteria which are to be considered by CFOs to assess an individual's eligibility to hold a firearms licence.

This includes assessing whether or not an individual has been convicted of certain *Criminal Code* offences, has been treated for mental illness, has a history of violent behaviour, or is the subject of a prohibition order against possessing firearms.

The Act also specifies that an individual is only eligible to hold a licence if they have successfully completed the necessary firearms safety courses.

The Act solely authorizes CFOs to make licensing eligibility determinations. Pursuant to Section 98 of the Act, these powers, duties and functions are formally delegated by the CFO to CFP Firearms Officers (FOs).

To ensure compliance with the *Firearms Act*, firearms licence holders are continuously screened to assess their eligibility to remain licensed.

If a PAL holder is involved in an event which could affect their eligibility (as defined by section 5 of the *Firearms Act*), it is reported by law enforcement via the Canadian Police Information Centre (CPIC) and sent to the relevant provincial CFO for review.

An event can also be registered by individuals using the CFP's 1-800 number or by the courts with the issuance of a Firearms Prohibition Order. A CFO is authorized to investigate the incident to determine if the client remains eligible to hold a licence.[27]

In addition, the RCMP's Firearms Internet Investigations Support Unit (FIISU)[28] conducts open-source internet investigations regarding firearms licensing, renewal and continuous eligibility. This means they search social media and other online sources for any information about PAL licence holders and criminals alike.

These investigations assist the CFO in determining a client's eligibility to possess (or continue to possess) a firearms licence.

"*Client*" is anyone with a firearms Possession and Acquisition Licence.

The Missing Link

The current system is focused entirely on individuals willing to comply with Canada's myriad laws and regulations to legally own a firearm.

Nothing in the *Firearms Act* or *Criminal Code* addresses individuals who are not "clients" of the Canadian Firearms Program and who violate Firearm Prohibition Orders.

Remember former RCMP Commissioner Bill Baker's words to Garry Breitkreuz almost two decades ago?

> "If someone is prohibited from having a firearm in the country they are no longer effectively covered by the *Firearms Act*. The *Firearms Act* only deals with people who own, possess, and use firearms. Firearms officers would have no authority to collect information from somebody who is not a client of the program."

Violent criminals get a total pass.

Nobody checks on them to ensure they remain compliant with their Firearms Prohibition Order. Nobody even knows where they live, since there is no legal requirement for anyone to track or check on these offenders.

Only in the minds of imbeciles does this system make any sense.

Chapter 4

Management of Sexual and Violent Offenders Units (MOSOVO)

The United Kingdom devotes teams of police officers to Management of Sexual and Violent Offenders Units (MOSOVO). The sole job of these units is to track offenders and ensure they comply with their protection orders.

The College of Policing explains:[29]

> Protecting the public is the responsibility of all police officers and staff working in the police service, but the police can't achieve this alone. Chief and senior officers are responsible for creating the structures that support the multi-agency coordinated approach that is crucial to ensure that the risk posed by sexual offenders, violent offenders and PDPs is managed appropriately and effectively.

Managers in charge of response policing should ensure that intelligence is used to equip patrol and response officers with the relevant information they need to fulfill their roles in the monitoring and management of such offenders.

All officers and staff must understand that their observations and knowledge, properly recorded, help to inform the intelligence picture and ensure that offenders comply with conditions placed upon them.

Individual police forces are given latitude on how they configure and staff their individual MOSOVO unit.

When staffing each unit, the focus is on finding officers who can deal with the complex issues that come with managing violent and sexual offenders and should have the skills, motivation and capacity required for the job.[30]

The College of Policing has developed training specific for police officers responsible for managing sexual and violent offenders. They also encourage joint training across police, probation and prison services, which benefit personnel from all three services.

Emphasis is placed on risk assessments, policies and procedures to ensure the safety and welfare of staff working in these units, and all decisions must be justifiable, but the focus of this program is to reinforce the offender's capacity to manage and control their own behaviour.

Each police force has a similarly wide latitude for managing case workload, which ensures each force is able to tailor their management unit to their own unique and specific needs.

Workloads relating to offender management must be manageable. The assessment of what constitutes a reasonable number of cases to manage must include a scrutiny of the risk level ratios (very high, high, medium or low) being managed by case officers. The current model practiced in force suggests that a maximum of 20 per cent of the caseload should be of a high risk level.

This is essential for the safety and welfare of officers, for resilience during periods of staff absence (e.g. sickness, annual leave, cover, vacancies and other absences) and for ensuring effective and proactive management of offenders. Workloads should take into account the:

- size of the geographic area
- population
- number of approved premises in the area
- number and type of offenders and PDPs requiring management.

There should be clear and auditable managerial scrutiny of these arrangements, undertaken regularly and in a timely manner.

Can you imagine the benefits to public safety if we slapped all 247 individuals (and counting) on my growing list of Firearm Prohibition Order violators[31] with an automatic five-year prison term?

The benefit to public safety would be real, tangible and measurable.

If only Canada's federal government cared more about implementing measures to keep Canadians safe instead of virtue-signalling about public safety while implementing measures that don't.

Chapter 5

Harm Prevention Orders: An Alternative to Firearm Prohibition Orders

The current Firearm Prohibition Order system is not designed to enhance public safety.

It's designed solely to provide the RCMP Canadian Firearms Centre with information to revoke Possession and Acquisition licences from current licence holders.

Canada needs a new system for registering, tracking and imposing compliance measures to ensure violent offenders who are prohibited from possessing firearms and other weapons obey the terms of those orders.

Under current Canadian law, there is no way to accomplish these public safety measures.

We need to start over with a new system – Harm Prevention Orders – that give police the authority to ensure compliance while giving judges the freedom to apply any (or none) of the available measures in court.

First, legislation must be introduced to Parliament to create a "Violent Offender Registry" for those convicted of violent criminal offences.

This could be modeled after our existing National Sex Offender Registry and would require the creation of a new section in Part XV, Special Procedure and Powers, of the *Criminal Code* similar to the existing notification requirements in Section 490.018 (1) for sex offenders.

The Commissioner of the Royal Canadian Mounted Police would be responsible for maintaining a new Violent Offender Registry just as they are responsible for maintaining the current National Sex Offender Registry.

The key element of any conviction requiring registration in the Violent Offender Registry is "violence."

While it is currently a criminal offence to possess firearms when your Possession and Acquisition Licence expires, there is no criminal intent nor is there a violent element to this offence. These individuals would not be eligible for inclusion in a new Violent Offender Registry.

Second, legislation must be introduced to allow police to search the registered individual and their place of residence to ensure compliance with their prohibition orders. This should be written to withstand a Charter challenge using the provision in Section 1:

> "subject only to such reasonable limits prescribed by law as can be demonstrably justified in a free and democratic society."[32]

Ensuring individuals with a violent criminal history do not possess weapons is a "demonstrably justified" restriction on a person's Charter rights.

Third, federal funding must be provided to create police units whose sole responsibility is ensuring compliance for registered violent offenders in their jurisdiction. These units would be modeled after the United Kingdom's highly successful Management of Sexual and Violent Offenders Units.

Chapter 6

Canada's Sex Offender Registry

Canada's National Sex Offender Registry (NSOR) was never designed for public safety or allowing parents to know if a sex offender is living in their neighborhood.

Its sole purpose is to assist police in locating suspects living near a specific crime scene.[33]

> "The Government of Canada, in partnership with the provinces and territories, created the NSOR to provide rapid access by police to current and vital information on convicted sex offenders."[34]

Public Safety Canada says there are no plans on making the registry available to the public.

Unlike the United Kingdom system, at no point does Canadian law require the registered sex offender to submit to random checks or any other supervision beyond reporting to their parole officer.

While Canada's *Sex Offender Information Registration Act* (SOIRA)[35] makes it mandatory for all persons convicted of sexual crimes to be registered in a database administered by the RCMP, that requirement may not survive a constitutional challenge.

In a ruling released on October 24, 2016, Madam Justice A.B. Moen struck down the mandatory registration of sex offenders as unconstitutional in R v Ndhlovu, 2016 ABQB 595.[36]

On June 19, 2018, Alberta's Court of Appeal of overturned Justice Moen's declaration.[37]

Until that appeal is heard, the law mandating all sexual offenders register with the government remains in force. Ultimately, it may come down to the Supreme Court of Canada to decide whether registering a convicted sex offender violates their constitutional rights.

Whether the Supreme Court values an offender's rights over public safety remains to be seen. They may choose not to hear the case at all.

The remedy to this is Section 1 of the Charter of Rights and Freedoms, as I described earlier, just as it would for a new Violent Offender Registry.

What follows are the requirements currently in place for registering sex offenders. As you will see, these requirements map nicely onto the new framework suggested for registering violent offenders with Firearm Prohibition Orders.

Current Sex Offender Registration Requirements

Anyone convicted of a sexual offence who fails to comply with an order to register or provinces false information

> is guilty of an offence and liable[38]

> > (a) on conviction on indictment, to a fine of not more than $10,000 or to imprisonment for a term of not more than two years, or to both; or
> > (b) on summary conviction, to a fine of not more than $10,000 or to imprisonment for a term of not more than two years less a day, or to both.

Section 490.018 (1) identifies who shall be notified of the requirement for an individual to register themselves in the National Sex Offender Registry.[39]

> **490.018** (1) When a court or appeal court makes an order under section 490.012, it shall cause

> > (a) the order to be read by or to the person who is subject to it;
> > (b) a copy of the order to be given to that person;
> > (c) that person to be informed of sections 4 to 7.1 of the *Sex Offender Information Registration Act*, sections 490.031 and 490.0311 of this Act and section 119.1 of the *National Defence Act*; and
> > (d) a copy of the order to be sent to
> > > (i) the Review Board that is responsible for making a disposition with respect to that person, if applicable,
> > > (ii) the person in charge of the place in which

that person is to serve the custodial portion of a sentence or is to be detained in custody as part of a disposition under Part XX.1, if applicable,
(iii) the police service whose member charged that person with the offence in connection with which the order is made, and
(iv) **the Commissioner of the Royal Canadian Mounted Police.**

The RCMP Commissioner is already responsible of registering sex offenders. They would likewise, under the proposed system, be responsible for registering violent offenders with prohibition orders.

Registered sex offenders must, within 7 days, report:[40]

- any change in their main or secondary addresses
- any change in their given name or surname
- after they receive a driver's licence
- after they receive a passport
- any change in their employment or volunteer information

Registered sex offenders must also report any absence from their main or secondary residence of seven days or more.

Designated Offences and Registration Requirements

The list of 68 *designated offences* for which registration is mandatory is found in the *Criminal Code* Section 490.011(1).[41]

Section 5(1) of the *Sex Offender Information Registration Act* lists the data an individual must give the government when registering:[42]

> 5 (1) When a sex offender reports to a registration centre, they shall provide the following information to a person who collects information at the registration centre:
>
>> (a) their given name and surname, and every alias that they use;
>> (b) their date of birth and gender;
>> (c) the address of their main residence and every secondary residence or, if there is no such address, the location of that place;
>> (d) the address of every place at which they are employed or retained or are engaged on a volunteer basis — or, if there is no address, the location of that place — the name of their employer or the person who engages them on a volunteer basis or retains them and the type of work that they do there;
>>
>>> (d.1) if applicable, their status as an officer or a non-commissioned member of the Canadian Forces within the meaning of subsection 2(1) of the *National Defence Act* and the address and telephone number of their unit within the meaning of that subsection;

(e) the address of every educational institution at which they are enrolled or, if there is no such address, the location of that place;
(f) a telephone number at which they may be reached, if any, for every place referred to in paragraphs (c) and (d), and the number of every mobile telephone or pager in their possession;
(g) their height and weight and a description of every physical distinguishing mark that they have;
(h) the licence plate number, make, model, body type, year of manufacture and colour of the motor vehicles that are registered in their name or that they use regularly;
(i) the licence number and the name of the issuing jurisdiction of every driver's licence that they hold; and
(j) the passport number and the name of the issuing jurisdiction of every passport that they hold.

In addition, the Act states the RCMP will:[43]

(a) register without delay in the database only the name of the police service and the following information relating to the person who is subject to the order:

(i) their given name and surname,
(ii) the number that identifies a record of fingerprints collected from them under the *Identification of Criminals Act*, if such a record exists,
(iii) every offence to which the order relates,
(iv) when and where the offence or offences were committed,
(v) when and where the person was convicted of, or found not criminally responsible on account of mental disorder for, the offence or offences,

(vi) the age and gender of every victim of the offence or offences, and the victim's relationship to the person,

(vi.1) the person's method of operation in relation to the offence or offences, if that information is available to the person who registers information,

(vii) the date and duration of the order, and

(viii) the court that made the order; and

(b) ensure that the registration of the information is done in a manner and in circumstances that ensure its confidentiality.

Chapter 7

Potential Challenges

The constitutional challenge of Canada's Sex Offender Registry could spell trouble for any legislative program for registering and checking on violent criminal offenders subject to a Firearm Prohibition Order.

At issue are the offender's right to privacy and to be free from unreasonable searches.

My position is any person convicted of violent criminal offences and who is subjected to a Firearm Prohibition Order has abdicated those rights.

The rights of law-abiding Canadians should always outrank the rights of those individuals with a proven track record of endangering public safety.

Simply put, in this instance, the rights of a few proven criminals should never outweigh the rights of the many good Canadians who obey the law.

Part 8:

Contact Your Elected Officials

If you, like me, want to see violent criminal offenders tracked and checked to ensure compliance with their Firearm Prohibition Orders, please write to the Minister of Justice and the Minister of Public Safety and demand they introduce legislation to reform Canada's Firearm Prohibition Order system.

Send them a copy of this report, as it spells out in clear language how we can truly improve public safety instead of continuing to pay lip service to the idea.

The Honourable David Lametti
Minister of Justice and Attorney General of Canada
284 Wellington Street
Ottawa, Ontario K1A 0H8
Email: mcu@justice.gc.ca

The Honourable Bill Blair
Minister of Public Safety
House of Commons
Ottawa, Canada K1A 0A6
Email: ps.ministerofpublicsafety-ministredelasecurite-publique.sp@canada.ca

Then contact your Member of Parliament and ask them to advocate for this reform as well. You can find their contact information on the Parliament of Canada website:

https://www.ourcommons.ca/members/

Thank You For Reading

Thank you for reading this policy book.

I hope you found value in the explanations provided, the conclusions drawn throughout, and the recommendation to create a new Violent Offender Registry and special police units whose sole responsibility is to ensure compliance with Firearm Prohibition Orders.

If you have any questions, concerns, comments or suggestions for improvement, you can reach me through the contact form on ChristopherDiArmani.org.

Yours in Liberty,

Christopher

Christopher di Armani
ChristopherDiArmani.com

Appendix 1

Firearm Prohibition Order Position Statements of Canada's Major Firearm Organizations

Canadian Shooting Sports Association (CSSA)[44]

People, not objects, commit crime.

While many groups campaign against legal guns and legal gun ownership, we know firearms are harmless unless a person with evil intent picks it up and uses it to commit an evil act.

That's why we're pushing the government to strictly monitor over 443,000 people courts deem too dangerous to possess guns, not the 2.2 million who the RCMP people investigated and deemed trustworthy of firearm ownership.

If so-called advocacy groups are as concerned about public safety as they claim to be, we urge them to join us in calling on our government to take action against the 443,000 individuals with Firearm Prohibition Orders (FPOs) registered against them.

From 2014-2018, 5,550 criminals already prohibited from possessing firearms were arrested for violating their Firearm Prohibition Orders.

In November 2019 alone, we found news reports of 41 criminals arrested for violating their existing Firearm Prohibition Order, along with numerous other charges. These individuals were previously banned from possessing firearms by the courts.

Write or call Minister Bill Blair today and politely demand he introduce legislation immediately requiring that every person with a Firearm Prohibition Order registered against them be held (at least) to the same standard as federally-licenced, RCMP-vetted firearm owners.

Demand those with Firearm Prohibition Orders registered against them be tracked daily in CPIC, just like licensed firearm owners.

Demand those with Firearm Prohibition Orders registered against them be forced to report change of address to the police or be subject to 2 years in prison, just like licensed firearm owners.

Instead of ignoring Canada's most violent offenders like many so-called advocacy groups insist, let's crack down on them instead.

Canadian Coalition for Firearms Rights (CCFR)

The CCFR does not have a specific policy on firearm prohibition orders though our licensing policy and organizational philosophy supports the following statement.

We believe in law and order. This means freedoms are to be enjoyed by the law abiding with the least amount of interference by the state while criminals should feel the full weight of it.

Much of the current effort of licensing could be replaced with a stronger system of firearm prohibition orders. Focusing more on keeping firearms out of the hands of those who ought not have them realizes a greater net benefit to public safety while treating law-abiding citizens with the respect they have earned.

via email

National Firearms Association (NFA)

The NFA supports tracking violent offenders.

We do not support licensing, registration of firearms or the tracking of innocent people, which are hallmarks of the current failed system.

via email

Appendix 2:

A Primer on Canadian Firearm Legislation

Full Disclosure: I'm biased.

- I like guns.
- I like hunting.
- I like plinking on the shooting range.
- I like occasionally winning shooting competitions.
- I used to teach the Canadian Firearms Safety Course as well as the Canadian Restricted Firearms Safety Course.
- During my 18-year career in the movie industry, part of my duties included training actors to handle guns appropriately for their character while maintaining a safe environment on set at all times.

In other words, I know a little bit about guns, how to use them safely, and how to pass that knowledge on to others.

My goal here is to pass a little of my knowledge on to you.

What You Will Learn

First, I will provide a brief and general overview of Canada's firearm classification system for those unfamiliar with Canada's firearms control legislation.

Second, I'll walk through the process of obtaining your Possession and Acquisition Licence (PAL) and your Restricted Possession and Acquisition Licence (RPAL).

Third, I will explain why the shooting sports are one of the safest activities in Canada – not according to me, but according to the insurance companies who sell liability insurance (and profit handsomely from it).

Fourth, I'll discuss why guns in the hands of bad people are always a problem – and why firearms in the hands of federally-licensed, RCMP-vetted individuals seldom are.

Fifth, I will encourage you to attend a sport shooting facility near you. I will encourage you to ask them for a tour of their facility and have them explain how the range operates to ensure everyone's safety.

Section 1: Canada's Firearm Classification System

1. **Non-Restricted Firearm** – these shotguns and rifles can be used for hunting, target shooting and shooting sports competition. They may be taken out into the bush and used for hunting and/or target shooting, or taken to a government-approved shooting range for target shooting.

3. **Restricted Firearm** – these firearms, most handguns and some rifles and shotguns, can only be used for target shooting and shooting sports competition. They must be taken to and from a government-approved shooting range and may only be used for those purposes.

4. **Prohibited Firearm** – all automatic firearms (like the military AK-47 or M-16), some semi-automatic rifles and shotguns, and illegally-modified guns like sawed-off shotguns and any handgun with a four-inch or shorter barrel and handguns designed to discharge a 25 or 32 calibre cartridge.

For more information, please visit the RCMP's Classes of Firearms page:

https://www.rcmp-grc.gc.ca/en/firearms/classes-firearms

Section 2: Canada's Firearm Owner Licencing System

The process to legally possess firearms in Canada is costly, both in time and money. Anyone wishing to legally own guns must pay for firearm safety training courses and all license application fees for which the total combined cost is usually between $400 and $500.

From the time you begin the process until you receive your Possession and Acquisition Licence card in the mail can be three or four months, and sometimes longer.

It is **not** a fast process.

Safety Courses

Both firearm safety courses are typically be completed in a weekend – two full days of learning basic firearm safety concepts like ACTS and PROVE, as well as how to safely handle a variety of firearms using hinge, bolt, pump, lever and semi-automatic actions.

The Four Vital ACTS of Firearm Safety

- Assume every firearm is loaded.

- Control the muzzle direction at all times.

- Trigger finger must be kept off the trigger and out of the trigger guard.

- See that the firearm is unloaded – PROVE it safe.

How to PROVE a Firearm is Safe

- Point the firearm in the safest available direction.

- Remove all cartridges.

- Observe the chamber.

- Verify the feeding path.

- Examine the bore.

License Application Fees

If you want to own Non-Restricted firearms (PAL), the licence application fee is $61.32.

If you want to own Restricted firearms (RPAL), the licence application fee is $81.76.

For more information, please see the RCMP's Service Fees page: https://www.rcmp-grc.gc.ca/en/firearms/chang-es-service-fees

The Licensing Process

The RCMP's Firearm Owner Licensing page (https://www.rcmp-grc.gc.ca/en/firearms/licensing) says:

- A firearms licence shows that the licence holder can possess and use firearms.

This statement from the RCMP means a firearms licence holder has successfully:

- Completed the Canadian Firearms Safety Course;

- Passed both the written and practical tests for the Canadian Firearms Safety Course;

- If they want to own handguns or other Restricted class firearms, they completed the *Canadian Restricted Firearms Safety Course* and passed its written and practical exams;

- Submitted an *Application for a Possession and Acquisition Licence Under the Firearms Act*, along with proof they've passed the CFSC (copies of course exams);

- Passed an RCMP background check where your references are called, your current and former conjugal partners are contacted, and the RCMP found no reason why you should not be permitted to possess firearms. (Typically, this means you have no criminal record or history of violence.)

If you pass all these requirements, the RCMP's Canadian Firearms Program will issue your Possession and Acquisition Licence and, once the licence is in your possession, you may legally acquire a firearm.

Section 3: The Shooting Sports are Among the Safest Sporting Activities in Canada

The primary reason to visit a shooting range is to see for yourself how ordinary Canadians safely and legally use firearms.

Statistically, shooting ranges are one of the safest places on earth. While this sounds completely illogical, insurance companies do not make moral decisions about firearms. They care about one thing and one thing only – making money.

Insurance companies make money by charging more in insurance premiums than they pay out in claims.

The more dangerous an activity, the higher the insurance premiums are to cover that activity because there are more claims.

For just $45 per year, you can obtain $5,000,000 of primary liability insurance for all your shooting activities in Canada.

https://christopherdiarmani.com/go/cssa/

Compare this to your vehicle's liability insurance. From the statistical perspective of insurance companies, driving a vehicle is dangerous and sport shooting is not.

For just $95 per year, you can also purchase legal defence insurance should you ever be charged with a firearms offence. This insurance covers up to $250,000 per claim and $1,000,000 per year.

https://christopherdiarmani.com/go/fld/

One of the downsides of Canada's stringent firearm control system is the law is extremely complex and confusing, even for judges and Crown prosecutors.

The average police officer doesn't stand a chance, not when the *Criminal Code* is over 1,000 pages long.

As a result, police will generally seize the firearm, arrest and charge the person with it, and let the judge sort it out. This is not a statement against police. They simply don't have the time or the resources required to fully understand every page of the *Criminal Code*.

If you choose to own firearms, $95 per year is awfully cheap peace of mind. It's also more proof this insurance company doesn't pay out much in legal fees each year. If they did, they could never offer to cover $250,000 of legal fees and expenses per claim.

Section 4: Guns in the Hands of Bad People are Always a Problem

When people with bad intentions pick up a gun, nothing good comes from it. We see the proof of this – week in and week out – in cities like Toronto, Montreal and Vancouver. It's not confined to big cities. Smaller cities like Edmonton, Saskatoon and Winnipeg also have far more violence than anyone wants to see.

I can't recall the last time I made it through an entire week without hearing about a shooting somewhere in our country. Almost without exception, the source is the same – bad people with illegal guns shooting at other bad people in an attempt to violently impose their will on others.

These shootings are fueled by drug dealers and gangs doing what drug dealers and gangs always do – protect their turf by violence.

These are not the licensed gun owners I discussed at the top of this article. These are violent criminals, often with long criminal records already, and they don't care about ordinary people like you and me.

The awful tragedy we just witnessed in Nova Scotia was no different. This was a man with a long history of violence who, one terrible day, took his illegal guns and went on a murderous rampage and killed everyone he came in contact with.

The uncomfortable reality of Canada's firearm laws is they focus on the law-abiding – on the people willing to take the safety course, on the people who can pass an RCMP background check – not on the violent criminals responsible for 99.9% of all the shootings.

A Firearm Prohibition Order is a restriction placed on criminals convicted of violent offences. This restriction can last for 5 years, ten years or for the rest of the person's life.

In 2018, the latest year for which the RCMP published the numbers, Canada had 459,538 individuals prohibited from possessing firearms.

On average, 29 people are arrested every month who are in illegal possession of firearms in violation of their pre-existing Firearm Prohibition Orders. These are just the ones I can find easily using a Google keyword search.

The true number is probably much higher based on an Access to Information Request by Dennis Young, which showed an average of 1,110 people are arrested for violating their existing Firearm Prohibition Orders.

These are the people who our system should be addressing but does not, an issue the Canadian Shooting Sports Association addressed in their commentary "Court Orders Can't Stop Criminals From Getting Illegal Guns":

https://cssa-cila.org/court-orders-cant-stop-criminals-from-getting-illegal-guns/

We need to focus our precious police and court resources on the people responsible for the carnage, not on the people who aren't.

Section 5: Visit a Sport Shooting Facility Near You

The primary reason to visit a shooting range is to see for yourself how ordinary Canadians use firearms legally and safely.

Most shooting ranges are happy to show you around and walk you through their safety procedures. Just give them a call, make an appointment, and then see what legal gun ownership and shooting ranges are all about.

It's a world vastly different from what you see portrayed in the newspapers or the evening news, but I don't want you to take my word for it – I want you to experience this for yourself.

If you need assistance locating a sport shooting facility near you, please contact me and I'll do my best to point you to a facility near you.

https://ChristopherDiArmani.org

EndNotes

1   https://www.rcmp-grc.gc.ca/en/audit-the-canadian-fire-arms-program-continuum-eligibility-firearms-licensing

2   https://www.publicsafety.gc.ca/cnt/cntrng-crm/gn-crm-frrms/index-en.aspx

3   https://www.cbc.ca/news/politics/trudeau-montreal-massa-cre-speeches-1.5386610

4   https://www.fraserinstitute.org/blogs/trudeau-governments-buy-back-gun-program-likely-a-multi-billion-boondoggle

5   https://ipolitics.ca/2016/12/22/how-bad-is-canadas-recidi-vism-problem-nobody-knows/

6   https://www.ncbi.nlm.nih.gov/pmc/articles/PMC4472929/

7   https://www.rcmp-grc.gc.ca/en/2018-commissioner-fire-arms-report

8   https://christopherdiarmani.com/firearm-prohibition-order-vi-olators/

9   https://dennisryoung.ca/2019/09/26/statscan-viola-tions-of-weapons-prohibition-orders-2014-2018/

10   https://www.change.org/p/justin-trudeau-shouldn-t-police-know-where-these-bad-guys-with-guns-live

11   https://www.foxbusiness.com/money/rioters-minneso-ta-bar-firefighter-life-savings

12   https://globalnews.ca/news/6996027/minneapo-lis-george-floyd-death-protests/

13   https://www.theatlantic.com/health/archive/2020/06/why-peo-ple-loot/612577/

14   https://www.ctvnews.ca/world/cars-burned-buildings-ran-sacked-as-protesters-across-u-s-clash-with-police-1.4961627

15   https://www.stltoday.com/news/local/crime-and-courts/retired-police-captain-shot-to-death-at-st-louis-pawn-shop-in-slaying-caught-on/article_d482138c-0224-5393-bd87-9898bebb3fd1.html

16   https://www.merriam-webster.com/dictionary/insane

17   https://laws-lois.justice.gc.ca/eng/acts/c-46/page-25.html

18   ibid

19   ibid

20   ibid

21   https://laws-lois.justice.gc.ca/eng/acts/F-11.6/page-10.html#docCont

22   https://www.rcmp-grc.gc.ca/en/2018-commissioner-firearms-report#a6_1

23   https://www.ourcommons.ca/DocumentViewer/en/38-1/JUST/meeting-8/evidence#Int-1032110

24   https://dennisryoung.ca/wp-content/uploads/2016/07/RCMP-ATIP-Response-CPIC-Search-on-Name-Address-Vehicle-July-18-2016.pdf

25   https://christopherdiarmani.com/firearm-prohibition-order-violators/

26   https://www.rcmp-grc.gc.ca/en/audit-the-canadian-firearms-program-continuum-eligibility-firearms-licensing

27   https://www.rcmp-grc.gc.ca/en/2018-commissioner-firearms-report

28   ibid

29   https://www.app.college.police.uk/app-content/major-investigation-and-public-protection/managing-sexual-offenders-and-violent-offenders/

30   https://www.app.college.police.uk/app-content/major-investigation-and-public-protection/managing-sexual-offenders-and-violent-offenders/#roles-and-responsibilities

31   https://christopherdiarmani.com/firearm-prohibition-order-violators/

32   https://laws-lois.justice.gc.ca/eng/const/page-15.html#h-40

33   https://www.macleans.ca/politics/who-belongs-on-canadas-sex-offender-registry/

34   https://www.rcmp-grc.gc.ca/en/privacy-impact-assessment-national-sex-offender-registry-nsor

35   https://laws-lois.justice.gc.ca/eng/acts/S-8.7/FullText.html

36   https://www.canlii.org/en/ab/abqb/doc/2016/2016abqb595/201

6abqb595.html

37   https://www.canlii.org/en/ab/abca/doc/2018/2018ab-ca260/2018abca260.html

38   https://laws-lois.justice.gc.ca/eng/acts/C-46/page-125.html#docCont

39   https://laws-lois.justice.gc.ca/eng/acts/C-46/page-121.html?txthl=490.018#s-490.018

40   ·   https://www.rcmp-grc.gc.ca/en/sex-offender-management

41   https://laws-lois.justice.gc.ca/eng/acts/C-46/page-119.html#docCont

42   https://laws-lois.justice.gc.ca/eng/acts/S-8.7/FullText.html#h-445979

43   https://laws-lois.justice.gc.ca/eng/acts/S-8.7/FullText.html#h-446081

44   https://cssa-cila.org/violent-people-not-objects-commit-violent-crime/

www.ingramcontent.com/pod-product-compliance
Lightning Source LLC
Chambersburg PA
CBHW022007190326
41519CB00010B/1424